D0518219

DEMCO

# Perfumes, Scented Gifts & Other Fragrances

## Make Beautiful Gifts to Give (or Keep)

**KELLY RENO**

**PRIMA HOME**
**An Imprint of Prima Publishing**
3000 Lava Ridge Court
Roseville, California 95661
(800) 632-8676 • www.primalifestyles.com

PRIMA PUBLISHING and its colophon are registered trademarks of Prima Communications, Inc. GOOD GIFTS FROM THE HOME is a trademark of Prima Communications, Inc.

DISCLAIMER: THE EXPRESS PURPOSE OF *PERFUMES, SCENTED GIFTS & OTHER FRAGRANCES* IS TO PROVIDE SUGGESTIONS FOR A RECREATIONAL HOBBY. THE AUTHOR AND PUBLISHER DISCLAIM ANY WARRANTY OR GUARANTEE, EXPRESS OR IMPLIED, FOR ANY OF THE RECIPES OR FORMULAS CONTAINED HEREIN AND FURTHER DISCLAIM ANY LIABILITY FOR THE READER'S EXPERIMENTS OR PROJECTS. THE AUTHOR OR PUBLISHER DO NOT ASSUME ANY LIABILITY FOR ANY DAMAGES THAT MAY OCCUR AS A RESULT OF READING OR FOLLOWING ANY OF THE RECIPES OR FORMULAS IN THIS BOOK. THE PURCHASE OF THIS BOOK BY THE READER WILL SERVE AS AN ACKNOWLEDGMENT OF THIS DIS-CLAIMER AND AN AGREEMENT TO HOLD THE AUTHOR AND PUBLISHER HARMLESS FOR ANY MISTAKES THE READER MAY MAKE AS A RESULT OF FOLLOWING THE RECIPES AND FORMULAS IN THIS BOOK.

**Library of Congress Cataloging-in-Publication Data**

Reno, Kelly.
   Good gifts from the home: perfumes, scented gifts & other fragrances: make beautiful gifts
to give (or keep) / Kelly Reno.
      p.    cm. — (Good gifts from the home)
   Includes index.
   ISBN 0-7615-2341-3
   1. Perfumes.   2. Cosmetics.   3. Handicraft.   I. Title.   II. Series
TP983.R378 2000                                                    00-028543
688.54dc21                                                         CIP


00  01  02  03  04   HH   10  9  8  7  6  5  4  3  2  1

Printed in the United States of America

**HOW TO ORDER**

Single copies may be ordered from Prima Publishing, 3000 Lava Ridge Court, Roseville, CA 95661; tele-phone (800) 632-8676, ext 4444. Quantity discounts are also available. On your letterhead, include infor-mation concerning the intended use of the books and the number of books you wish to purchase.

**Visit us online at www.primalifestyles.com**

. . . . . . . . . . . . . . . . . . . . . . . . . . . . . . . . . . . . . . . . . . . . . . . . . . . . . . . . . . . . . . . . . . .

≣ This book is lovingly dedicated to my mother, Dixie Lee, a true Southern belle.

# CONTENTS

# ACKNOWLEDGMENTS

I WOULD like to give special thanks to a friend and fellow crafter, Maria Skala. This special lady helped me get started in natural fragrance crafting years ago. She unhesitatingly answered my questions and provided me with rare texts and valuable information when there was little data to be found on the subject.

I would also like to thank all of you who read and then create. Together we are establishing toiletry-making as a standard craft. Thank you for your continued interest and support, and for your spirit of adventure.

FRAGRANCE IS a thread woven throughout the fabric of our lives, intertwining reality and dreams. Simultaneously tangible yet magically intangible, it is captured in tiny bottles yet abundant in our ordinary surroundings.

The recipes in this book call for a wide variety of natural oils from plant sources, so you can create light, wholesome fragrances without using chemicals or synthetic substitutes

The art of creating natural fragrances lets you capture, in a bottle, those things that make you happy and smell pleasant to you. I hope that you enjoy the formulas.

# CHAPTER ONE

# Natural Perfumes

THE WORLD we live in is filled with scents and aromas, from flowers and spices to baking bread and freshly cut grass. Man has enjoyed these fragrances for thousands of years, but it wasn't until just three hundred years ago that we discovered how to capture the essences of nature in a bottle.

## The History of Modern Perfumes

Around 1705, a man named Johann Farina discovered that mixing essential plant oils with alcohol created a pleasant-smelling astringent useful for relieving minor pains. He named his product *cologne* after his hometown of Cologne, Germany. In 1709, during the Seven Years' War, French soldiers began calling this fragrant topical medicine *eau de Cologne.*

It was not long before *eau de Cologne,* brought home by returning soldiers, became popular throughout France. After all, since eighteenth-century European cities were foul-smelling places—piles of sewage and trash filled the streets—everyone wanted to wear cologne. In response to this demand, Johann Farina moved his perfumery to Paris. This was the start of the French perfume industry. Today's perfumes and colognes still follow Farina's original formula, which consists of fragrant oils in an alcohol base.

## Crafting Fragrances

A fragrance is any sweet-smelling, pleasing scent. Perfumes, eau de toilettes, colognes, and splashes are examples of modern fragrances. Designing your own natural fragrances is a wonderful way to express your creativity. Plus, you'll have a good time combining scents and creating new formulas.

### *Common Fragrance Frequently Asked Questions*

*Q. What is the difference between perfume, eau de toilette, cologne, and splash?*
*A.* Perfumes are the most concentrated fragrances. Eau de toilettes are half as strong as perfumes, and colognes are half as strong as eau de toilettes. Splashes, the lightest fragrances, are half as strong as colognes.

*Q. What is the difference between essential oils and perfume oils?*

*A.* Two types of oils are used in modern perfumery: essential oils and fragrance, or perfume, oils. Essential oils are all-natural oils that have been extracted directly from flowers, fruits, herbs, or spices. For example, when rose petals are crushed, oil is extracted from the crushed petals. We will only use these chemical-free oils in the recipes you'll find in here.

Fragrance oils, sometimes called perfume oils, are synthetic, or man-made, oils. Fragrance oils were developed in the 1920s to imitate fragrances that could not be extracted from natural sources. Strawberry fragrance oil is one example. Though strawberries have a delightful smell, you could squeeze every ounce of juice from a strawberry and not get a drop of strawberry-scented essential oil. Because of this, chemists have chemically simulated the fragrance of strawberries.

Essential oils are a natural way to fragrance perfumes, soaps, and bath products, and are different from potpourri and candle fragrance oils. Potpourri oils and candle fragrance oils can cause allergic reactions and should not be used in bath and body products.

## Fragrance Bases

Modern fragrances are a combination of oils, alcohol, and water. You may be surprised as you see in the following recipes that ordinary types of alcohol, such as grain alcohol, rum, and vodka, are the bases used most often. These types of alcohol are readily available to home crafters and are similar to the industrial types used by perfumeries. You may also be surprised to discover that the expensive store-bought perfumes that often run in the hundred-dollar ranges are nothing more than a few pennies worth of ingredients. It's the marketing and fancy packaging you're paying for. To create alcohol-free gel fragrances, substitute unscented aloe vera gel for the alcohol in the recipes.

## Storing Natural Fragrances

As I've discussed, essential oils are used to make the formulas in this book. You'll notice that each recipe calls for jojoba oil or tincture of benzoin. These fixatives extend the life of the essential oils and make the scent last longer. Keep in mind that the aroma of essential oils will fade when exposed to light. The best way to store perfumes that contain essential oil is in amber, cobalt, or other colored glass bottles because the dark colors keep them potent, but storing them in clear glass is not forbidden.

*❧ Warning: Once you've added essential oils to alcohol, do not drink it. Adding essential or fragrance oils creates perfume, which could be harmful if ingested. Alcohol and alcohol-based products are flammable; keep these products away from heat and flames.*

### Testing Fragrance Blends

To avoid wasting oils and alcohol, you can test your blends by dipping wooden toothpicks into your oils, then holding the toothpicks together and waving them under your nose. This is the next best thing to actually smelling the final blend. Here are specific directions:

1. Arrange your bottles of essential oils in a row.
2. Place an inverted foam cup in front of each bottle.
3. Label the foam cups to match the oils.
4. Dip the flat end of each wooden toothpick into each oil, then stick the pointed end of the toothpick into the appropriate foam cup. (Wooden toothpicks that are flat on one end and pointed on the other end work best.)
5. Once you have samples of each oil, tilt the cups so that the tips of the scented toothpicks are close together. Use your hand to waft the fragrance toward your nose.

6. Replace or add essential oil–saturated toothpicks until you find the best blend.

7. Store the scented toothpicks in sealable plastic bags and use a permanent marker to record the name and proportions of the fragrances directly on the plastic bag. This way you can use the information any time to create your actual fragrance.

*Example: Creating a fragrance blend of rose as the dominant fragrance with notes of cinnamon and clove.*

*Dip two or three toothpicks in rose oil, one toothpick in cinnamon oil, and one toothpick in clove oil. Insert the other end of each toothpick into a foam cup. (Dipping several toothpicks in rose oil and only one toothpick in each of the other oils keeps the fragrance proportions realistic.) To change the fragrance blend, change the ratio of rose-scented toothpicks to spice-scented toothpicks.*

## Clearing the Olfactory Senses

In Europe, perfume testers routinely sniff freshly ground coffee beans in between sniffing fragrance samples. The aroma of freshly ground coffee helps to cleanse the olfactory senses during fragrance testing. (This is similar to eating crackers to cleanse the palate when tasting wines.) When blending perfumes, you might want to keep a can of freshly ground coffee nearby.

## Equipment

Natural perfume making is a simple craft. Because it requires a minimal investment in equipment, you can easily do it in your home. Glass measuring cups, glass droppers, and several sets of metal measuring spoons are your main tools.

❧ *Use only metal measuring spoons and glass measuring cups because some essential oils may warp plastic. (Glass and metal utensils are also less likely than plastic to absorb fragrances from essential oils.) You'll also need wooden toothpicks and foam cups (if you plan to test your fragrance blends) and an assortment of decorative bottles for storing newly created fragrances. Clearly label your essential oils and alcohol, and store them nearby.*

Clean your equipment after each use. Essential oils are strong; the odors left from insufficiently cleaned equipment will affect your next fragrance. Rubbing alcohol and vodka make good cleaners for perfumery equipment.

Set aside a designated space to store your perfumery materials. This will keep your equipment organized and away from cookware and food.

........................................................................

*Organization*

Before making natural fragrances, clear a flat work area. I have an entire room in my home set aside for my oils and equipment. (My family and I have nicknamed it "the laboratory.") An easily cleaned surface such as a kitchen countertop works well. Do not use a polished wood surface such as a dining room table! Cover your work area with layers of newspaper or craft paper.

Wear an apron or old shirt. I'll never forget the time I dropped a bottle of clove oil on myself. It took weeks to rid my kitchen of the smell, and I had to throw away the blouse I was wearing. When making perfume, a little precaution can make a huge difference!

Keep a notebook and writing tool handy! Taking notes as you work is the easiest way to remember your formulas—especially if you're creating your own blends.

## Fragrances for Women

The following recipes showcase a variety of natural fragrances for women. The collection includes formulas for heady florals, sweet floral bouquets, and more.

❧ *Be considerate when wearing fragrances. Some people are sensitive—or even allergic—to fragrances, or they simply may not care for yours. Just a dab of perfume or a spritz of cologne is enough! Wearing too much of a fragrance is considered bad manners.*

........................................................................

# PERFECT DAY

*Like tranquil waters beneath an azure sky, this natural eau de toilette captures the beauty and spirit of a perfect day.*

    1 ounce Everclear grain alcohol
    10 drops jasmine essential oil
    10 drops tuber rose essential oil
    10 drops lavender essential oil
    2 drops sandalwood essential oil
    15 drops jojoba oil

Combine all ingredients in a glass measuring cup. Stir until well blended. Bottle.

. . . . . . . . . . . . . . . . . . . . . . . . . . . . . . . . . . . . . . . . . . . . . . . . . . . . . . . . . . . .

*As the foghorn sounds in the distance, the Lady in White drops her bouquet into the crashing surf. Softly, she calls out the name of her lost lover. As the ghostly fog wraps its tendrils around her, she fades from sight.*

> 1 ounce Everclear grain alcohol
> 15 drops wood rose essential oil
> 3 drops patchouli essential oil
> 10 drops jojoba oil
> 1 drop blue food coloring

Measure the alcohol in a glass measuring cup. Add the essential oils, jojoba oil, and blue food coloring. Stir gently until well blended. Bottle.

*Drop a few rhinestones into the bottle of this deep blue fragrance for a dramatic effect.*

. . . . . . . . . . . . . . . . . . . . . . . . . . . . . . . . . . . . . . . . . . . . . . . . . . . . . . . . . . . .

. . . . . . . . . . . . . . . . . . . . . . . . . . . . . . . . . . . . . . . . . . . . . . . . . . . . . . . . . . . . . . . . . . . . . . . . .

*This light, floral cologne is for all of us who remember when a smile from a stranger or a heartfelt compliment from a new love caused us to blush. An innocent fragrance inspired by nature.*

> 2 ounces Everclear grain alcohol
> 15 drops lemon essential oil
> 15 drops tangerine essential oil
> 10 drops wood rose essential oil
> 15 drops jojoba oil
> Red food coloring

Measure the alcohol in a glass measuring cup. Pour into a bottle. Add the essential oils and jojoba oil and shake gently until well blended. Lightly dip the tip of a toothpick into red food coloring, then swirl the toothpick in the cologne. Use just enough color to give this delicate fragrance a very light pink tint.

*Design a cute bottle for this fragrance by painting pale pink polka dots on a round, clear perfume bottle. (Use transparent glass paint.) Tie a blush-pink ribbon around the top of the bottle.*

. . . . . . . . . . . . . . . . . . . . . . . . . . . . . . . . . . . . . . . . . . . . . . . . . . . . . . . . . . . . . . . . . . . . . . . . .

· · · · · · · · · · · · · · · · · · · · · · · · · · · · · · · · · · · · · · · · · · · · · · · · · · · · · ·

🦡 *This warm, musky fragrance was inspired by the bouquet of earthy aromas found in nature. Warm essential oils are blended with a hint of sugar-dusted fruit to create this unique eau de toilette.*

½ ounce Everclear grain alcohol
½ ounce Bacardi 151 rum
20 drops jasmine essential oil
10 drops frankincense essential oil
10 drops bergamot essential oil
2 drops chamomile essential oil
2 drops sage essential oil
20 drops tuberose essential oil
¼ teaspoon jojoba oil

Measure the alcohol in a glass measuring cup. Add the essential oils and jojoba oil. Stir gently until well blended. Bottle.

· · · · · · · · · · · · · · · · · · · · · · · · · · · · · · · · · · · · · · · · · · · · · · · · · · · · · ·

## DREAMY

........................................................................

🌧 *Drift away in a beautiful daydream—above the cottony, snow-white clouds. This carefree perfume combines the enticing aroma of green herbal essences and soft florals.*

½ ounce Everclear grain alcohol
20 drops rose essential oil
15 drops jasmine essential oil
5 drops chamomile essential oil
2 drops cedarwood essential oil
¼ teaspoon jojoba oil

Measure the alcohol in a glass measuring cup and pour into a bottle. Add the essential oils and jojoba oil to the alcohol and shake gently until well blended.

🕯 *For perfect packaging, use glass etching cream to draw cloud shapes on a glass perfume bottle.*

........................................................................

## GARDEN

......................................................................

🌿 *This fresh perfume is fragrant like a wild garden. A blend of florals, fruit, and herbs creates a clean, natural scent.*

> ½ ounce Everclear grain alcohol
> 20 drops geranium essential oil
> 15 drops wood rose essential oil
> 10 drops clary sage essential oil
> 10 drops lemon essential oil
> 5 drops bergamot essential oil
> ¼ teaspoon jojoba oil

Measure the alcohol in a glass measuring cup and pour into a bottle. Add the essential oils and jojoba oil to the alcohol and shake gently until well blended. Bottle.

......................................................................

........................................................................

*This breezy, floral cologne is bold and fresh, yet subdued and classic. The scent of green herbs combined with a strong floral base is nicely complemented by a hint of English bergamot.*

    2 ounces Everclear grain alcohol
    10 drops rosemary essential oil
    20 drops lavender essential oil
    2 drops bergamot essential oil
    10 drops jojoba oil

Combine all ingredients in a glass measuring cup. Stir until well blended. Bottle.

........................................................................

........................................................................

*This deep, heady cologne combines the lovely aroma of orange with light green notes and a hint of patchouli. Glittering gold mica dust gives this fragrance the look of liquid metal.*

2 ounces Bacardi 151 rum
¼ teaspoon orange essential oil
3 drops chamomile essential oil
2 drops patchouli essential oil
¼ teaspoon jojoba oil
¼ teaspoon gold mica dust

Combine the rum, essential oils, and jojoba oil in a glass measuring cup. Stir until well blended. Add a pinch of gold mica dust and stir a bit longer. Pour into a perfume bottle. Shake gently before using.

........................................................................

........................................................................................

*The sky's the limit when you wear a hint of this elusive eau de toilette. You'll find a natural bouquet of aromas with the sultry blending of rose and exotic ylang ylang.*

    1 ounce Everclear grain alcohol
    15 drops rose essential oil
    10 drops ylang ylang essential oil
    3 drops patchouli essential oil
    15 drops jojoba oil

Combine all ingredients in a glass measuring cup. Stir until well blended. Bottle.

*To create an exotic perfume bottle for this fragrance, paint the outside of a clear glass perfume bottle with burgundy stain-glass paint. Use faux leaded glass paint to draw tiny stars on the bottle.*

........................................................................................

# TARTAN

...................................................................

*This classic eau de toilette was inspired by the beauty of emerald lands and the spirit that still lives within the threads of tartan fabrics.*

        1 ounce Everclear grain alcohol
        15 drops orange essential oil
        10 drops bergamot essential oil
        2 drops frankincense essential oil
        2 drops rosemary essential oil
        2 drops chamomile essential oil
        2 drops sage essential oil
        2 drops cedar essential oil
        ¼ teaspoon jojoba oil

Measure the alcohol in a glass measuring cup. Add the essential oils and jojoba oil and pour into a perfume bottle. Shake until well blended.

*Tie a tartan ribbon around the neck of this perfume bottle.*

...................................................................

........................................................

*This delicate, floral perfume, woven from an intricate blend of flowers, is perfect for holiday gift-giving.*

    ½ ounce Everclear grain alcohol
    20 drops lavender essential oil
    2 drops geranium essential oil
    2 drops neroli essential oil
    10 drops jojoba oil

Measure the alcohol in a glass measuring cup and pour into a small bottle. Add the essential oils and jojoba oil, then shake for a few minutes.

*A frosted glass perfume bottle is the perfect storage container for this wintry fragrance. Use glass-etching cream, available at craft supply or hardware stores, to make delicate snowflakes on the frosted glass.*

........................................................

# LOVE POTION

*Listen up, ladies! A scientific study was recently conducted at an American university to discover what natural fragrances men liked the best. The study concluded that a man's number one favorite aroma was lavender. Number two was—get ready for this—pumpkin pie! In honor of this scientific study, I've blended this unusual combination of scents into the world's first Love Potion. The fragrance is floral with warm, spicy notes, and has an extremely pleasing aroma. But wear Love Potion with caution—the results of this potent formula are not yet known!*

    ½ ounce Everclear grain alcohol
    ¼ teaspoon lavender essential oil
    2 drops cinnamon essential oil
    1 drop clove essential oil
    1 drop nutmeg essential oil
    15 drops jojoba oil

Measure the alcohol into a glass measuring cup. Add the essential oils and jojoba oil and pour into a perfume bottle. Shake until well blended.

℣ *This potion is a fun gift for single ladies. Add a pinch of red or pink polyester glitter, just for fun.*

..................................................................................

*This delicate eau de toilette is floral and feminine, yet has subtle, spicy notes that hint of something mysterious.*

>    1 ounce Everclear grain alcohol
>    15 drops wood rose essential oil
>    10 drops lavender essential oil
>    2 drops cinnamon essential oil
>    1 drop cedar wood essential oil
>    15 drops jojoba oil

Measure alcohol in a glass measuring cup and pour into a small bottle. Add the essential oils and jojoba oil, then shake for a few minutes.

..................................................................................

# PINK CHAMPAGNE SPLASH

• • • • • • • • • • • • • • • • • • • • • • • • • • • • • • • • • • • • • • • • • • • • •

*Step from the bath and reach for a bottle of bubbly pink! Turn every bath into a special celebration with this festive after-bath splash. Made with French mineral water and the finest faux champagne scent, this will delight and refresh your skin— and your spirits.*

      6 ounces Everclear grain alcohol
      2 ounces sparkling mineral water (French or domestic)
      15 drops pink grapefruit essential oil
      10 drops lemon essential oil
      10 drops jojoba oil
      1 drop red food coloring

Measure the alcohol and mineral water in a glass measuring cup, then pour into a bottle. Shake. Add the essential oils, jojoba oil, and food coloring. Shake vigorously until well blended.

*For fun, bottle this bath splash in a small champagne split or double the recipe and use a regular champagne bottle. When giving this splash as a gift, wrap the champagne bottle in a linen dinner napkin and tie with a pretty ribbon.*

• • • • • • • • • • • • • • • • • • • • • • • • • • • • • • • • • • • • • • • • • • • • •

## BRIGHT EYES

..............................................................

*Try this light, fresh body splash after your morning shower, or when you need a quick pick-me-up. The fruity, sweet aroma is made from a blend of florals and fruit.*

    1½ cups 100-proof vodka
    ¼ cup orange flower water
    ¼ teaspoon lime essential oil
    10 drops lavender essential oil
    10 drops orange essential oil
    ¼ teaspoon jojoba oil

Measure the vodka and orange flower water in a glass measuring cup. Pour into a bottle. Slowly add the essential oils and jojoba oil. Shake until well blended. Shake the bottle daily until the fragrance is clear.

..............................................................

## The Antique Perfume Collection

The fragrances in this collection have been lovingly adapted from formulas popular during the Victorian Era. Each fragrance captures the era's authentic romance and spirit.

## HEIRLOOM ROSE

........................................................................

𖤣 *This timeless perfume woven from cedar, cinnamon, and velvety roses is perfect for inspiring true romance. Its woodsy blend will take you to another time, another place.*

> ½ ounce Everclear grain alcohol
> 15 drops rose essential oil
> 10 drops wood rose essential oil
> 5 drops cedar essential oil
> 2 drops cinnamon essential oil
> 1 drop clove essential oil
> 15 drops jojoba oil

Measure the alcohol in a glass measuring cup, then pour into a small bottle. Add the essential oils and jojoba oil, then shake for a few minutes.

𖤣 *Blend your own combination of floral oils to create a personalized bouquet-in-a-bottle.*

........................................................................

**MASQUERADE**

. . . . . . . . . . . . . . . . . . . . . . . . . . . . . . . . . . . . . . . . . . . . . . . . . . . . . . . . . . . . . . . . . . . . . . . . . . . . . . . . . . . . . . . .

🐾 *Sweet, powdery floral essences bloom amid hints of enticing citrus and give this cologne an irresistible charm.*

> 2 ounces Everclear grain alcohol
> 20 drops orange essential oil
> 10 drops ylang ylang essential oil
> 5 drops wood rose essential oil
> 5 drops geranium essential oil
> 2 drops tangerine essential oil
> 15 drops jojoba oil

Measure the alcohol in a glass measuring cup, then pour into a small bottle. Add the essential oils and jojoba oil, then shake for a few minutes.

........................................................................

*This traditional fragrance was inspired by the beauty and charm of the Deep South. A dab of cologne behind the earlobes will make you long for a tall, cool glass of sugared iced tea while you sit on the back porch swing and gaze at twinkling fireflies off in the distance. Fiddle-e-fee!*

    1½ ounces Everclear grain alcohol
    ½ ounce pure vanilla extract
    10 drops clary sage essential oil
    5 drops jasmine essential oil
    2 drops sandalwood essential oil
    3 drops tincture of benzoin

Measure the alcohol and vanilla extract in glass measuring cups and pour into a small bottle. Add the essential oils and tincture of benzoin. Shake gently until well blended.

*Give your perfume bottle a summer bonnet! Use a hot glue gun to attach a miniature straw hat to the top of the bottle.*

........................................................................

# CAMEO BOUQUET

. . . . . . . . . . . . . . . . . . . . . . . . . . . . . . . . . . . . . . . . . . . . . . . . . . . . . . . . . . . . . .

*For nostalgia's sake, dab a few drops of this authentic, old-fashioned perfume behind your earlobes. You're sure to fall in love with this romantic bouquet of roses, lavender, orange blossoms, herbs, and spices.*

> 1 ounce Everclear grain alcohol
> 20 drops rose essential oil
> 15 drops lavender essential oil
> 5 drops orange essential oil
> 2 drops cinnamon essential oil
> 2 drops sage essential oil
> 1 drop clove essential oil
> ¼ teaspoon jojoba oil

Measure the alcohol into a glass measuring cup, then pour into a small bottle. Add the essential oils and jojoba oil. Shake vigorously until well blended.

. . . . . . . . . . . . . . . . . . . . . . . . . . . . . . . . . . . . . . . . . . . . . . . . . . . . . . . . . . . . . .

.............................................................................

🌿 *Vanilla, with its alluring properties, was used in Victorian love potions. This modest and innocent fragrance combines vanilla with the sweet aroma of ylang ylang oil and a hint of musky angelica, capturing the spirit of true romance.*

      2 ounces Everclear grain alcohol
      1 tablespoon pure vanilla extract
      15 drops rose essential oil
      5 drops ylang ylang essential oil
      1 drop angelica essential oil
      10 drops jojoba oil

Measure the alcohol in a glass measuring cup. Add the vanilla extract, then pour into a small bottle. Add the essential oils and jojoba oil. Shake vigorously until well blended.

🌿 *For a stronger vanilla aroma, drop a one-inch piece of a vanilla bean into the perfume bottle before adding the fragrance. (Vanilla beans are available in the spice section of larger grocery stores. The alcohol in the fragrance will preserve the bean.)*

.............................................................................

## THE PARLOR

· · · · · · · · · · · · · · · · · · · · · · · · · · · · · · · · · · · · · · · · · · · · ·

*Step into the parlor room and make yourself comfortable. This delicate, powdery perfume, with just a dash of spice, is the perfect fragrance to wear while sharing the latest news over a cup of tea or coffee.*

½ ounce Everclear grain alcohol
15 drops rose essential oil
10 drops chamomile essential oil
5 drops neroli essential oil
1 drop cinnamon essential oil
1 drop clove essential oil
¼ teaspoon tincture of benzoin

Measure the alcohol in a glass measuring cup, then pour into a perfume bottle. Add the essential oils and tincture of benzoin. Shake until well blended.

## Fragrances for Men

Most often, when we think of men's fragrances, bold, spicy, woodsy aromas come to mind. These natural, classic, old-time fragrances are more appealing than many synthetic, modern fragrances—especially to those who believe a man's fragrance should be subtly noticeable only at close range, rather than strongly linger for hours after he has gone. After all, an overwhelming man's fragrance is just as repellent as an overwhelming woman's fragrance. Because each person's body chemistry is unique, fragrances react differently on different people. This collection of fragrances for men offers a variety of clean, natural scents that are bound to please.

## OCEAN SPICE

· · · · · · · · · · · · · · · · · · · · · · · · · · · · · · · · · · · · · · · · · · · · · · · · · · · · · · · · · · · · · · ·

*This warm, classic fragrance is perfect for nestling by the fireside or venturing out along the beach. This cologne is adventurous, yet soft as a fisherman's knit sweater.*

> 2 ounces Everclear grain alcohol
> ¼ teaspoon tincture of benzoin
> 15 drops lime essential oil
> 5 drops cinnamon essential oil
> 1 drop clove essential oil
> 1 drop rosemary essential oil

Measure the alcohol in a glass measuring cup, then pour into a bottle. Add the tincture of benzoin and essential oils. Shake until well blended.

· · · · · · · · · · · · · · · · · · · · · · · · · · · · · · · · · · · · · · · · · · · · · · · · · · · · · · · · · · · · · · ·

## CLASSIC BAY RUM

*Bay rum tonic has been a popular men's cologne for more than one hundred years. This vintage formula has a warm, spicy aroma and works great as a light aftershave.*

½ cup Everclear grain alcohol
¼ cup light rum
⅛ cup orange flower water
½ teaspoon tincture of benzoin
⅛ cup dried bay leaves
¼ teaspoon orange essential oil
1 drop clove essential oil

Measure the alcohol, orange flower water, and tincture of benzoin in a glass canning jar and add bay leaves. Close the lid and shake well. Keep in a cool place for two weeks and shake jar daily. After two weeks, strain liquid into a bottle and add orange and clove essential oils. (This fragrance has higher water content than other fragrances and takes longer to mix.)

   *This nostalgic tonic makes a great Father's Day gift. Put it in an amber, cobalt, or decorated glass bottle for nice packaging.*

.........................................................................

*The Inuit believed that the dancing lights of the Borealis were the spirits of children playing in the heavens. The woodsy fragrances of this crisp, clean cologne blend together to create an effect as electrifying and unforgettable as those dancing lights.*

> 2 ounces Everclear grain alcohol
> 15 drops tangerine essential oil
> 15 drops wood rose essential oil
> 7 drops sandalwood essential oil
> 2 drops pine essential oil
> 15 drops jojoba oil

Measure the alcohol in a glass measuring cup, then pour into a bottle. Add the essential oils and jojoba oil. Shake until well blended.

.........................................................................

........................................................................

*Capture the spirit of the great outdoors with this woodsy, green eau de toilette for men. This fragrance is perfect for outgoing, athletic men, yet subdued enough for those who are more quiet and reserved.*

> 1½ ounces Everclear grain alcohol
> Green food coloring
> ½ ounce pure vanilla extract
> 10 drops frankincense essential oil
> 10 drops sandalwood essential oil
> 2 drops patchouli essential oil
> 10 drops jojoba oil

Measure the alcohol in a glass measuring cup. Dip the tip of a toothpick into green food coloring, then swirl the toothpick in the alcohol. Use just enough food coloring to give the fragrance a tint of green. Add the essential oils and jojoba oil. Stir until well blended. Bottle.

*Wrap a few strands of raffia around the top of the bottle for a natural, outdoors look.*

........................................................................

......................................................................

🐾 *Capture the lure of the unknown in a tiny bottle! Unleash the spirit for adventure that lies within each man! Exotic aromas blend with a hint of spicy cinnamon in this crisp, fresh, masculine cologne.*

    1 ounce Everclear grain alcohol
    15 drops cedar essential oil
    15 drops ylang ylang essential oil
    2 drops sandalwood essential oil
    2 drops cinnamon essential oil
    15 drops jojoba oil

Measure the alcohol in a glass measuring cup, then pour into a small bottle. Add the essential oils and jojoba oil. Shake until well blended.

......................................................................

# FOREST

*The dusky, green aroma of the forest meets imaginary cool rivers in this carefully composed cologne. A dash of* Forest *invokes a feeling of freshness when it is used—a sure cure for monotony.*

    1 ounce Everclear grain alcohol
    15 drops sandalwood essential oil
    5 drops clary sage essential oil
    2 drops pine essential oil
    10 drops jojoba oil

Measure the alcohol in a glass measuring cup. Add the essential oils and jojoba oil, then pour into a bottle. Shake until well blended.

..................................................................................

🜛 *Exotic frankincense and spicy rosemary, complemented by amethyst clusters of lavender blossoms, bring a sample of nature's finest treasures to this light eau de toilette for men.*

  1 ounce Everclear grain alcohol
  15 drops lavender essential oil
  5 drops rosemary essential oil
  5 drops frankincense essential oil
  15 drops jojoba oil

Measure the alcohol in a glass measuring cup. Add the essential oils and jojoba oil, then pour into a bottle. Shake until well blended.

..................................................................................

# Scented Gifts
# & Wardrobe Fresheners

ADDING A TOUCH of natural scent to gifts is a great way to create special presents for your friends and family. Giving a fragrant homemade gift sends a message to the recipient about how much you really care. When my little boy brings me a present he made, I'm always overwhelmed because I know that he crafted it with his own little hands, just for me.

In this chapter, you'll find several items that you may have seen in gift shops or department stores, and other items that are truly one-of-a-kind. Hopefully, these projects will inspire you to create personalized gifts for everyone on your list, for every occasion. Happy crafting!

## Potpourri

Add a touch of natural scent to your rooms, or give a gift that's perfect for almost any occasion, by creating some home-crafted potpourri. The recipes in this section offer some whimsical and money-saving ideas.

# POTPOURRI ENVELOPES

. . . . . . . . . . . . . . . . . . . . . . . . . . . . . . . . . . . . . . . . . . . . . . . . . . . . . . . . . . . . . . . .

*I'm letting the secret out about potpourri envelopes—you know, the ones that you buy in department stores for about seven dollars? If you've ever opened one, you might have wondered, what is this stuff? Well, the secret ingredient in those expensive sachet envelopes is a substance called vermiculite that's been perfumed with oil. Vermiculite are natural, mineral formations you can purchase in most garden supply departments (all garden supply stores carry it) for around $2 a bag! The vermiculite is lightweight and holds fragrant oils for a long time. In fact, many gardeners sprinkle a layer of vermiculite over flowerbeds because it soaks up water like a sponge.*

*Make your own sachets, just like the ones in the department stores, for mere pennies by following the simple instructions below.*

    1 cup vermiculite
    ¼ teaspoon any essential oil
    ¼ teaspoon jojoba oil

Measure the vermiculite into a bowl. Sprinkle essential oil and jojoba oil onto the vermiculite, one drop at a time. Stir well. Air dry overnight. The next day, stir again, then spoon into envelopes.

*Make your own envelopes from homemade paper and attach a pretty bow to the envelope.*

*Add scented vermiculite to your regular potpourri to extend the potpourri's fragrance life.*

## Pastilles

A wonderful way to scent clothing and linens, pastilles are tiny, solid fragrances made from wax. People have used these fragrant sachets for hundreds of years—most commonly to scent clothing in drawers.

# BEESWAX PASTILLES

. . . . . . . . . . . . . . . . . . . . . . . . . . . . . . . . . . . . . . . . . . . . . . . . . . . . . . . . . . . . . . . . . . . . . . . . .

🖐 *Essential oils and dried, fragrant botanicals are used to craft these little treasures.*

¼ pound beeswax
¼ teaspoon any essential oil
¼ teaspoon jojoba oil
1 to 2 tablespoons dried flowers, herbs, or spices (a mixture of lavender and
    cinnamon is nice)
Small candy molds
Tissue paper or thin cloth

Melt the beeswax in a double boiler, then remove from heat. Add the essential oil and jojoba oil and dried botanicals to the melted wax. Stir until blended.

Pour the wax mixture into several small candy molds. Let set for one hour.

Warning: *Wax melts quickly and is flammable. Do not overheat, and keep wax away from a direct flame. Remove the wax pastilles from the molds and wrap in tissue paper or thin cloth. Store in a cool, dry place.*

*(continues)*

. . . . . . . . . . . . . . . . . . . . . . . . . . . . . . . . . . . . . . . . . . . . . . . . . . . . . . . . . . . . . . . . . . . . . . . . .

*(continued from page 45)*

. . . . . . . . . . . . . . . . . . . . . . . . . . . . . . . . . . . . . . . . . . . . . . . . . . . . . . . . . . . . . . . . . . . . . . . . . . . . . . . . . . . . . . . .

If the fragrance of your pastilles begins to fade, simply melt and remold the pastilles. Just add more essential oil to the melted wax before remolding.

&( *Pastilles with a rose fragrance are especially nice for lingerie drawers, but use lavender essential oil and lavender buds to make classic linen drawer pastilles.*

. . . . . . . . . . . . . . . . . . . . . . . . . . . . . . . . . . . . . . . . . . . . . . . . . . . . . . . . . . . . . . . . . . . . . . . . . . . . . . . . . . . . . . . .

## Sachets

Before the days of scented laundry detergent and scented dryer sheets, potpourri-filled sachets were used to keep linens and clothing smelling fresh.

# LAVENDER HEART SACHET

..............................................................................

🖐 *Decorate a doorknob or dresser drawer with this delicate heart sachet filled with fragrant lavender blossoms.*

    2 squares of lavender silk or purple velvet (8 inches by 8 inches)
    Tailor's chalk
    Scissors
    Thread to match fabric
    Sewing needle
    1 cup dried lavender blossoms
    Low temperature hot glue gun
    ½ yard narrow gold braid trim
    1 pearl or jewel bead
    ½ yard sheer lavender ribbon

..............................................................................

Using a heart-shaped template or pattern, trace two heart shapes on a piece of fabric. Cut them out with scissors and pin together.

Sew a ¼-inch-wide seam around the heart, leaving a one-inch opening on one side. Turn the heart right side out and fill with lavender blossoms. Stitch the opening closed.

Glue the gold trim around the edges of the heart. Sew a pearl or bead onto the bottom point of the heart. Fold the ribbon into a loop long enough for the heart to hang from a doorknob or dresser drawer. Sew the ribbon to the top of the heart.

# HANDKERCHIEF DOLL SACHETS

.......................................................................

𝕎 *These cute sachets, made from lacy handkerchiefs, add a touch of delicate scent to your drawers. (Lacy handkerchiefs can be found in accessory departments at larger department stores, and are bestsellers at bazaars. Or, look for vintage handkerchiefs the next time you're out antiquing.)*

> 3 cotton balls
> Favorite perfume
> White lace handkerchief
> Ribbon (18 inches long by ¼ inch wide)

Spray the cotton balls with your favorite perfume until the balls are slightly moistened (about three sprays per ball). Let the balls air dry for a few hours.

Place the cotton balls in the center of a handkerchief. Gather the ends of the handkerchief together. To make a head and neck for the handkerchief doll, use the ribbon to tie a bow underneath the knob of cotton balls.

You can stitch or paint a face on the doll's head.

𝕊 *Make a set of sachets for a friend, using her favorite fragrance.*

.......................................................................

CHAPTER THREE

# Scented Gifts
# & Fragrance Sprays

ALTHOUGH SACHETS and potpourri have been used for hundreds of years
in the home, spray fragrances have only recently been widely used to freshen
homes. These all-natural room sprays are easy to use and provide instant freshness to linens, upholstery, and carpets.

## Scented Linen Sprays

Linen sprays were designed to spruce up bedding and linens without having
to hang the linens out to air. You can mist these sprays directly onto bedding,
draperies, and upholstery without staining the fabric.

.......................................................................

*Encourage overnight guests to have a peaceful night's rest. Mist their pillows and sheets with this delicate floral spray. Take this along with you when you travel.*

    ¼ cup 100-proof vodka
    1 teaspoon tincture of benzoin
    25 drops lavender essential oil
    5 drops wood rose essential oil
    5 drops eucalyptus essential oil

Measure the alcohol and tincture of benzoin in a glass measuring cup. Add the oils. Pour into a spray bottle and shake. Shake the bottle before each use. Hold the bottle 2 feet from fabrics, adjust the nozzle to a fine mist, and spray lightly.

*Add a combination of lime and peppermint essential oils to create a "clean sheets" spray.*

.......................................................................

## Scented Room Sprays

Deliciously fragrant and all-natural room sprays add charm and hospitality to every room in your home by enhancing the aromas that drift from your kitchen.

# SUMMER HARVEST ROOM SPRAY

........................................................................................

🖐 *Capture the aromas of a summer harvest and bring them inside with this delightful room spray.*

    ½ cup Everclear grain alcohol
    20 drops cinnamon essential oil
    15 drops rosemary essential oil
    10 drops lemon essential oil
    ¼ teaspoon jojoba oil

Measure the alcohol in a glass measuring cup. Add the essential oils and jojoba oil. Pour into a spray bottle and shake. Spray lightly around a room.

........................................................................................

# HERBAL ROOM SPRAY

*This fragrance captures the aroma of a green, herbal garden that you can use to freshen various rooms in your home.*

½ cup Everclear grain alcohol
15 drops rosemary essential oil
10 drops basil essential oil
3 drops dill essential oil
10 drops jojoba oil

Measure the alcohol in a glass measuring cup. Add the essential oils and jojoba oil. Pour into a spray bottle and shake. Spray lightly around a room.

## HOME ROOM SPRAY

*This inviting aroma of cinnamon and gingerbread magically turns the house into a home.*

> ½ cup Everclear grain alcohol
> 15 drops cinnamon essential oil
> 15 drops nutmeg essential oil
> 5 drops ginger essential oil
> 15 drops jojoba oil

Measure the alcohol in a glass measuring cup. Add the essential oils and jojoba oil. Pour into a spray bottle and shake. Spray lightly around a room.

# CHAPTER FOUR

# *Scented Gifts & Home Furnishings*

LOVELY LITTLE gifts with a hint of natural fragrance are always well received. Make a scented gift for a dear friend using his or her favorite essential oil.

..............................................................

*Turn on the switch when you switch on the light. These whimsical lamps combine the glow of a miniature lamp with the beauty of a fresh bouquet of flowers. When the lamp is lit, the colorful flowers resemble panes of stained glass.*

Silk flowers, approximately 30
Low-temperature hot glue gun
10 to 30 silk leaves
Miniature lampshade, white
Epoxy glue
Battery-operated candlestick lamp, base, and bulb
4-inch terra cotta pot or small, tin watering can
Dried moss (enough to fill the pot or watering can)
Essential oil, any floral such as rose or lavender

..............................................................

Remove the flowers from the stems. Use the glue gun to affix flowers and leaves onto the lampshade, arranging them as you go. When the outside of the shade is completely covered, use extra petals and leaves to fill in any gaps. Use the glue gun to affix about 10 more leaves around the white part of the candlestick lamp base.

*Important:* Leave a ⅛-inch space between the candlestick base and the bulb socket.

Glue the candlestick base to the inside bottom of the pot or watering can. Let set per instructions on the epoxy glue.

After the glue is dry, insert the candlestick, batteries, and light bulb into the candlestick base. Fill the pot or watering can with dried moss. Sprinkle a few drops of floral essential oil directly onto the moss. Place the shade on the lamp.

𐫵 *These little lamps make great gifts and are great conversation pieces.*

𐫵 *Dried moss, available at garden centers and craft stores, is a natural potpourri fixative and will make a few drops of essential oil last for a long time. Refresh as needed.*

. . . . . . . . . . . . . . . . . . . . . . . . . . . . . . . . . . . . . . . . . . . . . . . . .

🌿 *Miniature topiaries add a nice touch of green and make attractive place-card holders in your formal dining room. The tiny topiaries can also be placed around your home anywhere you want to add a touch of greenery and natural herbal fragrance; they look especially nice on fireplace mantles.*

Antique white acrylic paint
3-inch miniature terra cotta pot
Metallic gold acrylic paint
Low temperature hot glue gun
6-inch twig, narrow
3-inch foam ball
¼ cup dried moss
10 drops of any essential oil (rosemary or chamomile are nice)

. . . . . . . . . . . . . . . . . . . . . . . . . . . . . . . . . . . . . . . . . . . . . . . . .

Use antique white acrylic paint to cover all surfaces, inside and out, of a miniature terra cotta pot. After the paint dries, accent the rim with a few touches of gold paint.

When all the paint is dry, use the hot glue gun to affix one end of a narrow twig to the bottom of the pot. Make certain the twig is centered inside the pot.

Press a foam ball onto the top of the twig. Use the glue gun to completely cover the foam ball with dried moss.

Fill the pot to the rim with the remaining moss. Add 10 drops of essential oil to the moss in the pot. Although the scent will last a long time (moss is a natural potpourri fixative), it can be refreshed with additional drops of oil, as needed.

❦ *Do not add essential oil to the top of topiary. Essential oils eat away at the foam.*

❦ *Write a personalized message on the rim of the pot with a narrow black or olive green paint pen.*

❦ *Sell your miniature topiaries at a bazaar.*

........................................................................

 *Whimsical seashells collected during family beachcombing expeditions have always been special treasures. Simply turn your finds into delightful keepsakes by filling the seashells with fragrant, solid perfume. Here is a recipe you can use to make your own all-natural, solid fragrances.*

> 1½ teaspoons beeswax, grated
> 2 tablespoons jojoba oil
> 10 drops jasmine essential oil
> 10 drops lavender essential oil
> 4 flat, bowl-shaped shells, such as oyster shells (Be sure the shells are clean!)
> 2 squares of clear cellophane (approximately 9 inches by 9 inches)
> 2 white ribbons, approximately 18 inches long by ¼ inch wide

Measure the grated beeswax and jojoba oil in a double boiler. Use medium heat to melt the wax. As soon as the wax is melted, remove the boiler from the heat and stir in the remaining essential oils.

Pour the mixture into the two bottom halves of the seashells, filling the shells. Set aside for thirty minutes, or until the perfumed wax hardens. Position an unfilled shell half on top of each filled shell.

........................................................................

Place one set of shells on a square of cellophane. Fold up the corners of the square; tie a ribbon around the cellophane to hold the wrapping closed. Store your Seashell Perfume Solids in a cool, dry place until you are ready to give them to someone special as a scented gift.

Warning: *Wax melts quickly and is flammable. Do not overheat. Keep wax away from a direct flame.*

These solids have many variations:

🐾 For a whimsical touch, place a faux pearl inside the bottom shell before pouring in the perfumed wax.

🐾 Use 20 drops of your favorite essential oil to create your own personalized seashell fragrance.

🐾 For perfume-on-the-go, fill small screw-top jars, little tins, or empty powder compacts with fragranced wax.

🐾 Use lemon, orange, or mint essential oil and you have a tasty lip balm!

## POTPOURRI CAKES

*These sweet-smelling faux cake slices are easy to make, and cost less than fifty cents each. (Similar cake-slice look-alikes sell in gift shops for as much as $10.) Get creative! Use your old potpourri and dried garden botanicals to create these imaginative decorations.*

> Floral Foam
> Low temperature hot glue gun
> Dried flower petals, leaves, wood shavings, tree bark or vanilla beans, and
>      miniature pine cones (enough material to cover the floral foam)
> 1 dried flower blossom
> 10 drops essential oil of your choice
> 10 drops jojoba oil

Cut the floral foam into a triangle, in the general shape of a cake slice. Glue dried flower petals to the sides, back, and top of the floral foam. Overlap the dried petals until all surfaces are covered.

Next, cut either the bark or the vanilla beans into thin pieces. Glue the pieces of bark in a stripe across the middle of each side of the petal-covered floral foam. (The stripes represent cake layers.)

To create fluffy icing for the cake slice, glue wood shavings or miniature pine cones to the top and back of the petal-covered floral foam.

Top the cake slice by gluing a colored blossom between two leaves.

In a small dish, mix your essential oil and jojoba oil together and sprinkle a few drops on the cake slice. (Refresh the fragrance as needed by adding more essential oil.)

❦ *Arrange the cake slice on a fancy plate to complete the fragrant illusion.*

CHAPTER FIVE

# Scented Gifts for Bath & Bedroom

IN THIS section you will find aromatic delights for the bedroom and bath made with nature's finest fragrances.

# ROSY TOES SLIPPERS

..............................................................................

*These romantic slippers, covered with a bouquet of white roses, perk up spirits even on chilly, winter nights. Give these scented slippers, along with a bottle of Pink Champagne Splash, to yourself or to a friend!*

> 20 drops rose essential oil
> 1 pair white or pink terry-cloth slippers
> White silk roses, medium-size, approximately 50 (enough to cover tops of both slippers)
> Low temperature hot glue gun

Scatter 10 drops of rose essential oil on the top of each slipper. Gently rub the oil into the fabric.

..............................................................................

Remove the stems from the silk roses. Use the hot glue gun to affix the roses to the tops of the slippers. Arrange the flowers as you glue them onto the fabric.

After the slipper tops are completely covered with flowers, re-glue any loose petals.

*Instead of white roses, cover these slippers with any silk flower—lavender, carnation, pansy, or other favorite. Scent the slippers with your favorite essential oil.*

*White rose slippers make lovely bridal shower gifts. For pretty gift packaging, place the slippers back-to-back and tie together with a pretty ribbon that matches the flowers.*

# SCENTED NAIL POLISH

..........................................................................

✍ *Here's another way to enjoy your favorite fragrance. Add a hint of scent to your special nail polish.*

      1 bottle nail polish (clear or colored)
      3 drops of your favorite essential oil (Do not add more than 3 drops or
            the polish will not work properly.)

Remove the top from the nail-polish bottle. Add 3 drops of essential oil. Close the bottle and shake vigorously. Your scented nail polish is ready to use but the fragrance will not be noticeable until the polish is applied and has fully dried.

🖐 *This is a perfect stocking stuffer—a tangy fruit such as lemon or a perky peppermint scent is perfect for teenagers. Add a pinch of colored mica dust or polyester glitter for a hint of extra sparkle.*

..........................................................................

## Fragrant Bath Sets

These natural toiletries make perfect gifts for any occasion, and you can custom-coordinate their fragrances and give them as a matched gift set. Your friends won't believe you made these spectacular gifts!

## AFTER BATH SPLASH

. . . . . . . . . . . . . . . . . . . . . . . . . . . . . . . . . . . . . . . . . . . . . . . . . . . . . . .

👋 *Bath splashes help tone the skin while adding a subtle hint of fragrance.*

  ½ cup Everclear grain alcohol
  2 tablespoons aloe vera gel
  10 to 15 drops essential oil (your choice of fragrance)
  10 drops jojoba oil
  1 drop food coloring (your choice of color)

Measure the alcohol in a glass measuring cup. Add the gel, essential oil, jojoba oil, and food coloring. Pour into a bottle. Shake until well blended.

# BASIC BATH POWDER

........................................................................

𝕸 *Bath powder helps to absorb perspiration and leaves the skin feeling silky smooth.*

    ½ cup cornstarch
    2 tablespoons kaolin clay
    1 teaspoon orrisroot powder
    ¼ teaspoon Everclear grain alcohol
    10 drops essential oil (your choice of fragrance)

Measure cornstarch, kaolin clay, and orrisroot powder into a bowl. Stir until blended. Measure alcohol in a glass measuring cup. Add the oil to the alcohol. Stir until well blended. Add the alcohol/oil solution to the cornstarch/clay mixture, one drop at a time. Stir with a fork until no lumps remain. Let the powder air dry overnight. Stir again the next day. Pour the powder into a powder can or salt shaker. Store the powder in a cool, dry place when it is not being used.

........................................................................

## BATH & MASSAGE OIL

Luxurious bath and massage oils with dried flowers and herbs suspended in the oil make beautiful, unique gifts. Scented with your favorite fragrance, these oils are perfect to add to your bath or massage into your skin.

 8 ounces mineral oil or castor oil
 15 drops essential oil (your choice of fragrance)
 15 drops jojoba oil
 Dried flowers, herbs, or silk flowers (enough to arrange inside bottle)

Measure the mineral or castor oil into a bowl. Add the essential oil and jojoba oil. Stir until well blended. Place dried botanicals or silk flowers inside a glass bottle. Pour the oil mixture into the bottle and seal the bottle with a stopper or cork.

**₤** *To give your bottle of Bath & Massage Oil a finished look, dip the top of the filled, corked bottle in sealing wax. Tie a pretty ribbon around the neck of the decorative glass bottle (which you can purchase at an import or gourmet cooking shop). Make an instruction tag from pretty, homemade paper. Tie the tag to the bottle.*

# BASIC BATH SALTS

......................................................................

🖐 *Bath salts are used to tone and soften the skin.*

> ½ cup rock salt (the kind used with ice-cream makers)
> ½ teaspoon glycerin
> ¼ teaspoon essential oil (your choice of fragrance)
> ¼ teaspoon food coloring (your choice of color)

Measure the rock salt into a bowl. Add the glycerin, essential oil, and food coloring. Stir with a fork for about 5 minutes or until the salt crystals are evenly coated with coloring. Let the salts air-dry overnight. Store the salts in a sealed, moisture-free, glass container.

🥄 *To use bath salts, add 2 tablespoons to warm bath water.*

......................................................................

# CHAPTER SIX

# *Gift Wrapping*

WHAT FUN you can have restoring and decorating previously used perfume bottles! After all, the bottles used to store your fragrances should be as dazzling as the natural scents themselves.

## Recycling Old Perfume Bottles

I'm always searching for beautiful bottles for my concoctions. In my great searches I've discovered many tips: If you scour antique shops, garage sales, and second-hand stores for tiny, glass perfume bottles, you will soon have a nice collection.

A problem with old bottles is the old perfume smell and tattered paper labels. Here are easy ways to restore these beautiful bottles and turn them back into sparkling little gems.

### Removing Scents from Used Bottles

To remove the scent from an old perfume bottle, wash the bottle with hot, soapy water, then rinse well.

Next, fill the bottle with grain alcohol, vodka, or rubbing alcohol. Cap the bottle and shake it for a few minutes. Pour out the liquid. Repeat as necessary until the old scent is gone.

### Removing Ink, Gummy Labels, and Paper Labels

Sometimes a great bottle will have printing on the glass or have a sticky paper label. You can remove silk-screen writing on almost any bottle by lightly rubbing over the writing with a spongy nail buffer. Nail polish remover also works quite well for removing gummy labels and paint.

Remove paper labels by soaking the bottle in a pan of warm, soapy water. Once the label is loosened, peel it off the bottle. Remove any gummy residue with nail-polish remover.

### Decorating Perfume Bottles

You can decorate plain perfume bottles in many ways. Several examples are given in the fragrance recipes, and here are some more ideas.

🖐 Glue flat glass marbles onto bottle caps or stoppers.

🖐 Coat the outside of the bottle with stained glass paints.

🖐 Use faux stained-glass paint to trace over the flutes and designs on old bottles.

🖐 Use glass-etching cream to create frosted glass patterns on plain glass bottles.

🖐 Cut a letter stencil from masking tape, then use the glass-etching cream to monogram the bottle. Be careful not to drip glass-etching cream on your bottle where you don't want it. (Practice on an old piece of glass before applying designs to your bottles.)

🖐 Use stained glass paint to make handmade labels for the bottle.

🖐 Dip rubberstamps into glass paint and stamp the design onto the bottle.

🖐 Fasten tiny, metal charms or wire cages to the bottle with epoxy glue.

🖐 Mold fine chicken wire around a perfume bottle, then adorn the wire with glass beads.

🖐 Use a glue gun to attach a small, feathered angel or a pair of butterfly wings to the back of the bottle, giving it a whimsical look.

🖐 Tie a ribbon that coordinates with the perfume's theme around the neck of the bottle.

🐾    Wrap a perfume bottle in sheer fabric tied with a ribbon.

🐾    Dip a filled perfume bottle in wax to create a sealed, finished look. To do this, melt a small amount of colored beeswax, then dip the capped end of the bottle in the wax several times.

## Creating Decorative Gift Boxes

A decorative gift box adds a classy finishing touch to your fragrance gift. First, find a box that is the right size for your gift. Open the box flat and trace the box pattern onto a piece of colored card stock. Next, fold the card stock into a box shape and glue the new box together. To make a window in the card-stock box, cut an opening in the box lid, then glue a piece of clear plastic inside the lid.

## Storage and Shipping Tips

Here are several tips to keep your fragrances fresh and secure during storage or shipping.

🐾    Never store natural fragrances in plastic or vinyl bottles. Essential oils will weaken the plastic and may even eat through the bottle.

......................................................................

🐾    Always use glass bottles and containers. The best way to store fragrances made with essential oils is in amber, cobalt, or colored glass bottles. The colored glass keeps out sun and other light, which can make the scent fade.

🐾    Before mailing glass bottles, make sure the stoppers are fastened securely and the bottles are tightly sealed.

🐾    Always wrap glass bottles in bubble wrap, then nestle the bottles in packing material such as foam peanuts.

🐾    Mark the package *Fragile, Glass,* or *This End Up.*

......................................................................

# *Marketplace*

LOCATING THE ingredients you need to make fragrances can be quite a treasure hunt if you don't know where to look.

## Perfume & Toiletry-Making Supplies Available at Stores

The alcohols used as fragrance bases are located at most liquor stores. You can also find some floral waters in the cooking section of your grocery store. Glycerin, aloe vera gel, tincture of benzoin, and some essential oils are available in the first-aid section of drug stores. Bath and beauty shops, and some health-food stores, carry essential oils. Import shops carry new bottles, and antique bottles are readily found at antique stores and at flea markets. Of course, you can find your craft materials at most craft stores.

## Mail-Order Sources for Toiletry-Making Supplies

General Bottle Supply
1930 E. 51st St.
Los Angeles, CA 90058
(800) 782-0198
*This company offers a wide selection of glass, plastic, and perfume bottles. Call or write for a free catalog.*

Lorann Oils
P.O. Box 22009
4518 Aurelius Rd.
Lansing, MI 48909-2009
(800) 248-1302
*This company offers a wide variety of flavor oils, candy-making supplies, and essential oils.*

San Francisco Herb Company
250 14th St.
San Francisco, CA 94103
(800) 227-4530
*You can get your dried herbs, dried flowers, or potpourri ingredients here.*

Sunburst Bottle Company
5710 Auburn Blvd., Suite #7
Sacramento, CA 95841
(916) 348-5576
*Here you'll find a wide selection of glass, plastic, and perfume bottles. Send $2 for their catalog.*

Valley Hills Press
3400 Earles Fork Rd.
Sturgis, MS 39769
(800) 323-7102
*Order books about traditional soapmaking through this company.*

Victorian Essence
P.O. Box 1220
Arcadia, CA 91077
(888) 446-5455
Web site: www.Victorian-Essence.com
*This business provides one-stop shopping for the home toiletry crafter. Call or write for a free catalog. You can buy essential oils, perfume bottles, aloe vera gel, oils, soap molds, cosmetic clays, booklets on making toiletries, mica dust, powder containers, soapmaking supplies, unscented soap and shower gel bases, bottle labels, balm containers, and soapmaking kits for beginners.*

## Candlemaking Supplies

General Wax and Candle Company
P.O. Box 9398
North Hollywood, CA 91609
(800) WAX-STOR
Web site: www.genwax.com
*Through General Wax and Candle Company, you can access a full line of candle-making supplies, including molds, wax, additives, books, colors, fragrances, and beginner kits. Call or write for a free catalog or visit their Web site.*

# INDEX